KNOWING CHRIST

KATLEGO C. MALATSI

Printed in the Republic of South Africa

Acknowledgements

I want to appreciate and thank God for such a humbling opportunity to present a revelation He gave me. Thank you for the beautiful family You gave me Lord, I am absolutely nothing without You. A beautiful son, and his beautiful mother, I'm a blessed man indeed.

A special thanks to my beautiful and supportive wife. She's just a gift of God in my life. A God-fearing woman deserves to be praised. She deserves all the credit that is due her. She's my anchor from the Lord.

Thanks also to my bigger family at large; had they not been part of my life, I could have never come thus far. I couldn't ask for a better family. My friends, who are always nearby in my times of need, may the Lord extend a special blessing on them.

The Born Fire Ministries, thank you for believing in me, for trusting God through my life, most of all, for your continuous prayers and support. I thank God for you all. Amen.

Contents

Foreword iii

Introduction v

CHAPTER 1: **Christianity, A Relationship** 9

CHAPTER 2: **Self Identity** 22

CHAPTER 3: **Knowing Christ** 30

CHAPTER 4: **The Effects Of Knowing Christ** 37

    Peter the rock 40

    Geology 42

    Igneous Rock 44

    Sedimentary Rock 49

    Metamorphic Rock 55

Chapter 5: **The Benefit Of Testing** 62

Chapter 6: **Maturity and Responsibility** 68

Chapter 7: **Effective Life** 76

Foreword

From high school, after I received Christ in my life as my personal saviour, at the age of 16, I knew I was called to preach the Gospel. I started preaching to my peers and fellow students as a training ground for my upcoming work of preaching the Word. The Lord had to lead me through what I now call an In-service training for the ministry through the help of my fellow brothers and sisters who were there through those years to ensure that I grow in my calling. I also had the privilege of attending leadership workshops at the same time which contributed a lot to my growth.

However, it was only after I had finished my high school years that the Lord gave me the message of Knowing Christ, when I was revisiting my roots by preaching in high schools. The first time I presented the sermon on Knowing Christ was in HF Tlou High School, in Tlhabane, Rustenburg, with the company of Apostle L.M. Lephoi, in the year 2006. Since that time the Lord has grown me deeper into the understanding of how the knowledge of Christ should be the primary subject of every Christian's everyday life.

I believe this subject is manifold and broad, and through this book I believe God will grow every reader's understanding and personal relationship with God, by revealing more of what might be left out in this book. Thus said, it will not take me by surprise if this book triggers a vast release of other books closely related to it or even expanding to it. I believe there is more in every reader than just the reading of this book. I believe God will reveal great things through this book until more people feel and see the need to tell their side of the story.

Introduction

Throughout the generations Christianity has been portrayed in various diverse manners, influenced by the wave of events related to it. Nevertheless, this has not reduced the power of the Word of God in its application. It still remains true that when believed and acted upon, the necessary results are experienced. However, it is common amongst believers to wonder 'why am I going through this, why me, why now, when will it end?' and this book seeks to answer those questions in a rather intriguing way. A believer should always believe. Everything that happens to us as believers seeks to reveal the plan of God in our lives; this is the centre of a believer's faith.

As you read this book, it will become clear to you why God allows us to pass through our experiences, and why is it necessary for us to experience what we face in life. The Word of God is true when it says 'all things work together for our good' and this is the book you need to realise that you are not forgotten, you are not rejected, and neither are you forsaken. You are not cast out from God. You are still loved. God is still in control even when we don't see it. Everything that happens to us in life serves for one purpose, to reveal Christ in our everyday living.

CHAPTER 1:

Christianity, A Relationship

Towards the end of His ministry, Jesus told a parable that is commonly known as the parable of the Prodigal Son (Luke 15:11-32). To give a brighter picture to the story, the younger brother decided to demand his inheritance while his father was still alive. This is totally not acceptable because inheritance can only be in effect after the death of the father. Nevertheless, the father decides to adhere to the son's unlawful demand. Demanding his inheritance implied that he is no longer part of the family. By law he is independent and there is nothing that ties him to the family anymore. Everything that connected him to the family has been given to him. He is now independent. He is no longer under any control. Nobody is responsible for the decisions he makes. To a father who raises a son, this is both humiliating and insulting. By demanding his part of the inheritance, he is declaring that his father is of no use to him anymore; in fact he is as good as dead.

> *"...Inheritance can only be in effect after the death of the father"*

Knowing Christ

Since the boy decided to squander his possessions, he
lost everything. All his money and goods were lost. He
became as good as a slave. He never really learned how
to be economically wise. He did not know how to
generate income or manage what he had so everything
he had was lost. During the time of setback in his life,
when famine hit the land, jobs are scarce and friends are
far, he finds a job in a farm, where he has to take care of
pigs. There is not enough food for him and the
alternative becomes the food supplied for the pigs. He is
at the lowest moment in his life. While still experiencing
the reality of life, trying to figure out what to do, he
remembered that there is a place where he can get a
better job. A job that will not only pay him enough, but
will also see to it that he eats well and healthy. That
place is the place he is all familiar to. That is his former
home.

Knowing full well that he does not qualify to be called a
child in that house, he decides to go and ask for a job. He
decides that he would be a slave in his father's house. To
his surprise, the father has always been waiting for him.

He has never been rejected as a son. Irrespective of the insults and bad decisions he poured out on the father, he is still loved as a child. The father has always anticipated his coming. The father kept on believing that one day the boy will come to his senses. He kept on believing that he will learn a lesson that will make him realise how valuable family is. He believes the boy will learn to treasure relationships. The boy comes home and, as he had already resolved, he asks the father to treat him as a servant. But the father had a greater purpose, he had a greater standard. He had a son who came back home. He never lost his position as a son in the father's heart. Although by law he is required to be treated as a servant due to his poor decision, he is received as a son. His older brother insists on legal terms but the father refuses to adhere to that. He proves what the bible declares; *"...mercy triumphs over judgement"* (James 2:13).

> *"Although by law he is required to be treated as a servant due to his poor decision, he is received as a son "*

Knowing Christ

The founder and pastor of Excellence Ministries International (EMI), Apostle LNT Kgobokwe once defined the difference between Christianity and other religions in this manner: *"Religion is the system in which people seek and try to find God, but Christianity is a system in which God finds man, because God is not lost, people are."* Christianity, unlike other religions, is based on a relationship that people share with their God. Isaiah 1:18 makes this clear: *"Come now, and let us reason together, saith the LORD: though your sins be as scarlet, they shall be as white as snow; though they be red like crimson, they shall be as wool."* (KJV). God places a need for fellowship and communion with His

> *"Christianity, unlike other religions, is based on a relationship that people share with their God "*

people above everything. Acknowledging that sin is the primary driving force that separates Him from His people, He caters for the need by assuring us that He will wash our sins away, which implies that the most important thing is fellowship. Even sin cannot stop God in His attempt to fellowship with His wonderful creation of mankind. He takes the initiative to ensure that communication is established. He chooses to deal with the issue of sin Himself.

The need for God to fellowship with His people is seen even in the days of Moses, when God required sacrifices from the children of Israel. One of the most significant sacrifices was called the **"Atonement Sacrifice"** which was offered every year. In Leviticus 16, God gives the detailed procedure of the sacrifice, how it should be carried out. The word **"Atonement"** from the Easton's Bible Dictionary *"is simply at-one-ment, i.e., the state of being at one or being reconciled, so that atonement is reconciliation."* God is showing the children of Israel that He wants to be part of their lives by demanding that every year they present an offering of reconciliation. This sacrifice is purposed to keep the children of Israel *at-one* with God. The relationship between God and man that was lost in the Garden of Eden was restored by the death of Jesus Christ on the cross.

Jesus became the last, significant sacrifice that redeemed mankind back to God. This is declared by the book of Hebrews: *"Consequently, when Christ came into the world, he said, 'Sacrifices and offerings you have not desired, but a body have you prepared for me; in burnt offerings and sin offerings you have taken no pleasure.'"* (Hebrews 10:5-6 - ESV).

"The death of Christ on the cross was the price that was required to buy back the relationship between God and man"

Since the system of sacrifices demanded that blood should be shed in order for a relationship with God to be confirmed, God sent His only Begotten Son (John 3:16) to shed His pure blood that the system should be put to an end and a true relationship can be established, which not only limits God to one nation of Israel but that the whole world can share in fellowship with God through Christ Jesus our Lord. Paul says, about the redemption through Christ: *"Ye are bought with a price; be not ye the servants of men."* (1 Corinthians 7:23- KJV). The death of Christ on the cross was the price that was required to buy back the relationship between God and man. God was willing to pay the price and indeed He showed that the importance of fellowship surpasses His majesty, that He could even leave His throne on high just to bring us back to Himself.

> *"For every relationship, Love is the basis and if allowed to grow cold, the relationship is under thread of collapse"*

Jesus, in Revelation 2:4 tells John to address the church at Ephesus with these words: *"Nevertheless I have somewhat against thee, because thou hast left thy first love."* (KJV). For every relationship, Love is the basis and if allowed to grow cold, the relationship is under thread of collapse. Jesus makes it clear that the church has more than just a religion of rules with God but it is based on a relationship where God and man both express their love for each other. John says it this way: *"In this is love, not that we have loved God but that he loved us and sent his Son to be the propitiation for our sins."* (1 John 4v10 - ESV). In every love relationship, knowing the person we relate with is the most critical aspect which makes the relationship to grow strong.

Since God already knows us, the demand is placed on us to know God. In fact God makes it clear to us that beyond any shadow of doubt He knows all about us when He addressed Jeremiah: *"Before I formed thee in the belly I knew thee; and before thou camest forth out of the womb I sanctified thee, and I ordained thee a prophet unto the nations."*(Jeremiah 1:5 - KJV). God is our creator and He makes it clear that He created us and that there is nothing He does not know about us.

This means that for us to be saved, we encountered the Love of God which brought us to His kingdom. In Romans 2:4(b) Paul makes a remarkable statement when he says: *"...not knowing that the goodness of God leadeth thee to*

> *"When we see the Love of God for us, we become compelled to surrender ourselves to Him"*

repentance?"(KJV). When we see the Love of God for us, we become compelled to surrender ourselves to Him. It is His goodness to us that leads us to repentance. This process continues in our lives of Christianity and Paul highlights it in Romans 12:1 when he says: *"Therefore, I urge you brothers, in view of God's mercy, to offer your bodies as living sacrifices, holy and pleasing to God—this is your spiritual act of worship."*(NIV). It is only when we view the mercy of God that we are able to offer our bodies as living sacrifices. This shows that God's love has enough power to cause us to approach His throne with

> *"Without commitment from the two parties, it is impossible for the relationship to survive"*

confidence (Hebrews 4:16) and surrender our lives to Him.

Now that we see that God is the initiator of the relationship we have with Him, we are now responsible to do our part in order to maintain the flame of love in this relationship burning. A relationship is a two-way responsibility. Without commitment from the two parties, it is impossible for the relationship to survive. One person can do their best to keep a relationship alive but if the other person does not engage in their responsibility, that relationship will not last. God has done His part in the relationship. We need to take our place in our relationship with God and make sure that we know Him. The more of God we know, the more we find ourselves enjoying and growing in this relationship. Every one of us feels a need to be understood, especially by the person closest to us. In order to maintain a relationship, there has to be mutual understanding between us and God and since God knows all about us, we need to know Him and continually grow in knowing Him more.

When Jesus was approached by a multitude in Matthew 22, He received a question from a lawyer that was supposed to tempt Him. He asked: *"Master, which is the great commandment in the law?"*(Matthew 22:36). The following verses show the response of Jesus: *"Jesus said unto him, Thou shalt love the Lord thy God with all thy heart, and with all thy soul, and with all thy mind. This is the first and great commandment. And the second is like unto it, Thou shalt love thy neighbour as thyself. On these two commandments hang all the law and the prophets."*(Matthew 22:37-40 - KJV). What Jesus is saying to them is that the law was meant to maintain the relationship between God and man, and that relationship is established by love. If we want to associate with God, we need to base our relationship on love. From the words of Jesus we can see that this love is in a higher level. It is not just a partial love that is based on feelings; it is a love of total surrender, where our full commitment is required. God gave His all (Jesus, His Only Son) in order to establish this relationship. It is only fair that we give our all too.

So how much does God love us since He requires that we give our everything? David was puzzled by the love of God when he wrote: *"When I look at the sky, which you have made, at the moon and the stars, which you set in their places--- what are human beings, that you think of them; mere mortals, that you care for them? Yet you made them inferior only to yourself; you crowned them with glory and honor. You appointed them rulers over everything you made; you placed them over all creation: sheep and cattle,*

"God values us so much that He saw it fit for us to dominate the earth as He dominates the heavens"

and the wild animals too; the birds and the fish and the creatures in the seas. "(Psalm 8:4-8 - GNB). God values us so much that He saw it fit for us to dominate the earth as He dominates the heavens. Everything that He created was meant to sustain a human life on earth. This love did not end there but after man lost His authority over creation by breaking the commandment of God in the Garden of Eden, God sent Jesus to restore the order of His creation and bring back the relationship that we lost with Him. We owe God everything. We did not deserve His love but He saw it fit that He love us unconditionally and so it is fair that He demands our total attention in love.

CHAPTER 2:

Self Identity

After the war that claimed his father and grandfather's lives, a young boy was taken away from the city by a guardian who resolved to raise this boy as his own. She had to rush the boy out in fear that she might be killed together with the boy. Tragically, on her way while running, the boy fell down, crippling both of his legs. The boy was only five years old and so this caused him a permanent dysfunction of both his legs. His name was Mephibosheth (2 Samuel 4:4). The only thing this boy knew in his growing up is that David wants to kill him. With the assumption that David would want to get rid of everybody that belonged to Saul's house, the guardian kept him far away from the reach of David.

It came as a surprise some day, when David asked, *"Is there anyone still left of the house of Saul to whom I can show kindness for Jonathan's sake?"* Ziba referred to Mephibosheth, who had to be taken to stay in the palace with David (2 Samuel 9). As long as he was away from the palace, he did not know that he was destined for a place in royalty. He only knew David to be an enemy, not knowing that he is the gateway to a better life. Due to the covenant that David had wit Jonathan, Mephibosheth was a ruler in the new kingdom of David. He was to be given portions of the kingdom and a royal seat. Nevertheless this boy did not know who he really was supposed to be. False information had him running away from his breakthrough. Until David took him in, he was always going to believe that David wants to kill him. **And so with us, before we become believers, we thought God wants to punish us for our sins, until we come to know Him and realise that He always wanted to save us and give us the best in life.**

In order to establish a relationship with God, we need to discover our own identity in Him. God is our creator and we are His creation. He knows best who we are and what He created us to be. The best way to live our lives is to know what God thinks about us so that we can be the best that we can be. God is our source and the centre of our being. Without His plan for our lives we will always wonder around in dissatisfaction and a lack of fulfilment. Joseph Prince, senior pastor of New Creation Church said in one of his messages: *"Christianity is a lifestyle of receiving from beginning to end and those who are good receivers are also good givers."* Our ability to maximise our potential lies in our ability to receive the plan of God for our lives and carefully following Him in order to see this plan fulfilled in our lives.

I usually make an example with a motor car. The manufacturer knows the potential of his design and makes sure to sell it after a thorough check at the performance, in line with specifications. It will be disappointing for the manufacturer to pass his design one day and realise that it is used as a playground object for kids in a park. Knowing the capability of what he designed, how good it is, how fast it can run, how many passengers it can carry and how useful and handy it can become, it will be disappointing to see that none of those things are performed by the machine. That's exactly what happens when we do not know the plan of God for our lives. We perform things that are not within the range of our specifications. I can only imagine how God feels every time we fall in the trap of doing things He did not create us to do.

Paul makes an interesting statement when he addresses the people of Athens: *"For in him we live, and move, and have our being..."* (Acts 17:28 - KJV). This means that our proper identity is in God, our creator. God, through

> *"It is only in seeking Him that we are able to unlock the real identity of who we are"*

Jeremiah makes us aware that we need to lean on Him: *"For I know the thoughts that I think toward you, saith the LORD, thoughts of peace, and not of evil, to give you an expected end."* (Jeremiah 29:11 - KJV). The next three verses that follow afterwards talk about seeking God and the restoration that God brings as a result of seeking Him. It is only in seeking Him that we are able to unlock the real identity of who we are. Paul makes it clear when he addresses the Colossians: *"For you have died, and your life is hidden with Christ in God."* (Colossians 3:3 - GNB). This helps us to see why we need God to reveal our identity to us. If we died and our lives are hidden with Christ in God, the only way we can find our lives is to search Christ! This scripture will be explained in more detail on the coming chapter.

So what does God say about us? There are many ways God reveals our identity in His word. Although we may argue that the bible is general and therefore does not reveal the individual identity of a person, however, as already discussed in the previous chapter, God is personal and is therefore able to reveal Himself to us as individuals. It is through His word that we are able to identify His mind about us, and it is through a personal relationship that He is able to reveal our individual identity to us. Someone once said that *"the bible is like a mirror, in which we continually check ourselves if we are still intact."* As we grow deeper in our relationship with God, we also learn how God communicates with us. Jesus says about us: *"I am the vine, and you are the*

> *"As we grow deeper in our relationship with God, we also learn how God communicates with us"*

branches. *Those who remain in me, and I in them, will bear much fruit; for you can do nothing without me."* (John 15:5 - GNB). He helps us to understand that we need Him to such an extent that if we were to attempt to live without Him, we would be wasting our lives. Without Him our lives are meaningless and serve no purpose. As long as we are attached to the vine, we will be fed and nurtured and we will receive direct communication from the source. Whatever we can achieve without Him is still nothing.

The book of Psalms also confirms this by declaring: *"Unless the LORD builds the house, those who build it labor in vain. Unless the LORD watches over the city, the watchman stays awake in vain."* (Psalm 127:1 - ESV). So it is clear that we can never find our true identity unless we allow God to be the basis of our identity. Unless the Lord builds our lives, we are living lives of vanity and emptiness. Unless the Lord watches over our lives, we will never be safe.

> *"Unless the Lord watches over our lives, we will never be safe"*

David stretches it further when he said: *"The LORD is my shepherd; I shall not want."*(Psalm 23:1 - KJV). He is pointing out that the relationship he has with God is that of a sheep and a shepherd. Since sheep are vulnerable creatures, they rely on the shepherd for both direction and protection. He acknowledges God to be His source of survival. The only way we can function to the maximum capacity of our design is if we can allow God to partner with us and become the driving force of our lives.

CHAPTER 3:

Knowing Christ

Knowing Christ

"But whatever were gains to me I now consider loss for the sake of Christ. What is more, I consider everything a loss because of the surpassing worth of knowing Christ Jesus my Lord, for whose sake I have lost all things. I consider them garbage, that I may gain Christ and be found in him, not having a righteousness of my own that comes from the law, but that which is through faith in Christ—the righteousness that comes from God on the basis of faith. I want to know Christ—yes, to know the power of his resurrection and participation in his sufferings, becoming like him in his death, and so, somehow, attaining to the resurrection from the dead."
Philippians 3:7-11 (NIV)

In general, this is the most important thing ever in Christianity. We cannot claim to believe in someone we do not know. It is critically important for every Christian to can answer the question: *"Who is Christ?"* However, there is somewhat significance in knowing Christ

"A dead body has no control of its own; it depends on the living being that can control it"

personally that unleashes the power of God in a Christian's life. Just like mentioned in the previous chapter, the bible gives a general view that each and every one of us should be able to grasp. This is not the end of it though, because just like we need a personal experience with God that reveals our individual identity, we need a personal revelation of Christ that will unlock the power of God in our lives as individuals. Just like God used to reveal Himself in different ways to different people in the Old Testament, so we also need a fresh individual revelation of Christ in our lives.

What Paul said to the Colossians: *"For you have died, and your life is hidden with Christ in God."* (Colossians 3:3 - GNB), simply tells us that our true identity is not clearly revealed to us as yet. A dead body has no control of its own; it depends on the living being to control it. A friend of mine, also my colleague, Pastor D.A. Mathala said in one of His sermons: *"Imagine if God could show* us everything about our lives from the beginning to the end, what we will go through before we reach our destiny. Who of us would still want to proceed in that way? Most of us would want to pull off and change directions." John also admitted this in his book, 1 John 3:2 when he said: "My dear friends, we are now God's children, but it is not yet clear what we shall become. But we know that when Christ appears, we shall be like him, because we shall see him as he really is." (GNB). The scriptures of the bible tell us all we need to know about Christ. Since it is not yet clear who we are, we are left with a quest for searching for our identity and the only way to find it is to find Christ, because as Paul said, we are dead and our lives hidden with Christ in God. I suggest then that finding Christ will help us find ourselves.

> "I suggest then that finding Christ will help us find ourselves"

It seems as though God purposefully placed the scriptures together such that as we continually search to know more about Him, we may be able to find our own identity as well in the process. It is like scattered pieces of a puzzle which can only give a clear picture when rightfully joined together. After all it makes sense why God would hide our identity such that if we want to find it we need to search Christ first. Christ is the only one who has ever lived a perfect

"The knowledge of Christ is the key that unlocks the power to a Christian living"

life that models a relationship with God. He is not only the initiator of Christianity but He is the perfect model of the lifestyle itself. He proclaimed in John 14:6 *"I am the way, the truth, and the life: no man cometh unto the Father, but by me."* (KJV). This means that He not only brings access to the father through faith in Him, but He also shows us how to walk in this new life of fellowship and communion with God the Father. The knowledge of Christ is the key that unlocks the power to a Christian living.

One of the people that show us the effect of having a personal revelation of Christ in the bible is Peter. It is quite interesting that the bible clearly shows Peter as a person who was inquisitive, and quick to act. He would often question what Christ is saying or doing and also want to get involved. When Jesus washed His disciples' feet (John 13v5-12), Peter almost refused to allow Jesus to wash His feet until Jesus had to explain the importance of that act. He then required more than just the feet to be washed but Jesus had to come through again with an explanation. When he sees Jesus walking on water (Matthew 14:25-33), he did not want to accept that it is only Jesus who can walk on water. He demanded to join Him.

Perhaps it is this character of Peter that put him in a position of being ready to receive a fresh revelation from heaven. Jesus said in Matthew 5:6 *"Blessed are they which do hunger and thirst after righteousness: for they shall be filled."* (KJV). Every time we approach God with the need to receive from Him, we build an atmosphere in which God is able to pour out a fresh revelation in our lives. It is only when we show our hunger and thirst that God can fill us. It is not possible to fill a cup that is already full. Peter always showed a need to be filled by indicating that he has room for more from Jesus. He was ready to receive; he believed that there are no limits. Later in Acts, we learn that he was uneducated but his desire to receive overwhelmed his uneducated status. He was more eager to know than the others and willing to stand for what he believed. It is no surprise that he was one of the pillars of the early church (Galatians 2:9 - NLT). When Jesus was arrested, it is the same Peter who cut off one of the soldiers' ear (John 18:10). He was willing to fight for what he believed, even if it meant a physical fight. Irrespective of who we are, what kinds of people we may be and where we may be coming from, we all have the ability to receive the revelation of Christ necessary to make us the kinds of people God designed us to be.

CHAPTER 4:

The Effects Of Knowing Christ

"Knowing God without knowing our own wretchedness makes for pride. Knowing our own wretchedness without knowing God makes for despair. Knowing Jesus Christ strikes the balance because he shows us both God and our own wretchedness."
— Blaise Pascal

Peter in his second letter says: *"As we know Jesus better, his divine power gives us everything we need for living a godly life. He has called us to receive his own glory and goodness!"* (2 Peter 1:3 - NLT). Somehow Peter recognised that the power to live for God and to serve Him does not come from us but from God Himself. Our ability to please God is dependent on how much of Jesus we know. Our knowledge of Jesus is equipment to obedience and godly living. Paul says in the book of Romans: *"Because the carnal mind is enmity against God: for it is not subject to the law of God, neither indeed can be."* (Romans 8:7 - KJV). Since we were all separated from God by sin, we are all trained to rebel against God from childhood. It is what we do naturally. God can never demand from us what He did not give to us since He is the one who created us. I heard a friend of mine say: *"It is not your responsibility to live a holy life; more so, it is your response towards God's ability that enables you to live a holy life!"* This means that the ability is drawn from God through the knowledge of Jesus and this ability, as Peter says, comes with the power required to carry out the lifestyle.

"God can never demand from us what He did not give to us since He is the one who created us"

Peter is showing us that somehow God places in Christ the power we need to live a Godly life. The only way we can ever please God is if we search deeper and deeper in the person of Christ until the power to please God is unleashed in us. Remember what Paul said to the Colossians: *"For you have died, and your life is hidden with Christ in God."* (Colossians 3:3 - GNB). The reality of the matter is that we do not know who we ought to be. Paul says: *"Therefore if any man be in Christ, he is a new creature: old things are passed away; behold, all things are become new."* (2 Corinthians 5:17- KJV). A new creation is something that has never existed before. This means that we are unfamiliar to this new change of life. That is why God has to prepare everything we will ever require in Christ. John takes it to another level when he says: *"Whosoever abideth in him sinneth not: whosoever sinneth hath not seen him, neither known him."* (1 John 3:6- KJV). He says that the knowledge of Christ diminishes the ability for us to sin against God. If we claim to know Him yet continue to live sinful lives then we have only scratched the surface of who He is because a deeper knowledge of Jesus equips us to reject anything that displeases God.

Peter the rock

Let us look at Peter's encounter of the revelation of Christ and how it impacted him. One day while Jesus was with His disciples He decided to challenge them. He asked them: *"...Whom do men say that I the Son of man am?"* (Matthew 16:13- KJV). This question was not much of a problem to answer since Jesus was famous and they used to hear people talking about Jesus. But then the challenge came when He turned to them and asked: *"But whom say ye that I am?"* (Matthew 16:15-KJV). This was a confrontational question that brings them to the awareness that they might have walked with Jesus for some time but that does not automatically mean that they know Him. In fact when I read this portion of scripture, I imagine a time gap before Peter responded. The answer was not of this world and actually nobody among them had any logical response to the question. Peter, with his character managed to receive a fresh download of a revelation from God and replied: *"Thou art the Christ, the Son of the living God."* (Matthew 16:16- KJV).

> *"It took a revelation from the father to know who Jesus is"*

Jesus knew for a fact that Peter could not have figured out who He is by any human intellect. It took a revelation from the father to know who Jesus is. This became so exciting to Jesus that He said: *"Blessed art thou, Simon Barjona: for flesh and blood hath not revealed it unto thee, but my Father which is in heaven. And I say also unto thee, That thou art Peter, and upon this rock I will build my church; and the gates of hell shall not prevail against it."* (Matthew 16:17-18 - KJV). Previously when Jesus talked about the rock, he was giving a parable that describes obedience to His words when He said: *""Therefore whosoever heareth these sayings of mine, and doeth them, I will liken him unto a wise man, which built his house upon a rock:"* (Matthew 7:24 - KJV). No matter the disaster that was encountered by the house of this man, being it the rain, the floods or the wind, the house managed to stand.

Geology

"Ever since God created the world, his invisible qualities, both his eternal power and his divine nature, have been clearly seen; they are perceived in the things that God has made..." (Romans 1:20 - GNB).

God is so concerned about us that He does not end His revelation in the confines of the bible alone; He made His glory to manifest through His creation as well. This means that God is not limited and cannot be contained by human intellect; He far surpasses what we can imagine. Proverbs 6:6-8 indicates the wisdom of God hidden in creation: *"Lazy people should learn a lesson from the way ants live. They have no leader, chief, or ruler, but they store up their food during the summer, getting ready for winter."*(GNB). Perhaps if we can view the words of Jesus to Peter in a Geological point of view, this can help us see the wisdom of God hidden in His creation.

> *"This means that God is not limited and cannot be contained by human intellect"*

In order to better understand what Jesus is saying to Peter, let us study and observe the rock according to Geology. First of all, a rock is defined as *"the hard material of the earth's crust"* (Oxford Dictionary). This tells us that a rock is characterised by hardness. Naturally speaking, anything hard has to go through some kind of process which in many instances is hostile and unpleasant. Another thing that hard things have in common is that they develop with time. Geology teaches us that there are three types of rocks, which are named and classed according to their source of formation. In other words, a rock is classed according to how it came to being. The three types of rocks are: **Igneous Rock, Sedimentary Rock,** and **Metamorphic Rock.** Let us look at them in more details.

Igneous Rock

The word Igneous is derived from the Latin word igneous meaning **'of fire'** (Wikipedia). Igneous rocks are originally from the burning magma within the surface of the earth. This magma has a tendency of erupting, which means coming up to the surface of the earth in the form of volcano. Immediately the magma reaches the surface of the earth, cooling starts to take place and this magma material starts cooling down and solidifying to form a rock. Quite commonly, it is believed that the origin of most of the minerals found on earth originate from this magma. The continuous burning and finally cooling of this molten material finally forms a rock which results in the most useful things that benefit mankind.

God says through Isaiah: "*When you pass through the waters, I will be with you; and through the rivers, they shall not overwhelm you; when you walk **through fire** you shall not be burned, and the flame shall not consume you.*" (Isaiah 42:2 - ESV). Even though it is not pleasant to admit and uncomfortable, God often allows us to go through things that push us to the ultimate product that He wants us to be. He says when we walk through the fire it shall not burn us. This means that He allows the fire

"...He allows the fire to cross our paths for a purpose"

to cross our paths for a purpose. There is nothing that the devil can do to us except that which is allowed by God, for the benefit of His children. Paul indicates this in his letter to the Corinthians: *There hath no temptation taken you but such as is common to man: but God is faithful, who will not suffer you to be tempted above that ye are able; but will with the temptation also make a way to escape, that ye may be able to bear it."* (1 Corinthians 10:13 - KJV). The purpose is simply this: **The fire is not meant to destroy us, it is meant to produce a rock out of us!**

Peter had to go through some trying times and for some time it seemed like he is no longer the same rock Jesus referred to. In actual fact, four verses after Peter was called a rock, he is now referred to as Satan: *"Jesus turned around and said to Peter, 'Get away from me, Satan! You are an obstacle in my way, because these thoughts of yours don't come from God, but from human nature.'"* (Matthew 16:23 - GNB). As quick as he was to catch a revelation from God, so quick he was to lose it and follow his human nature. He was not immune to error. The same occurred with David, the second king of Israel and the greatest king that ever ruled the nation of Israel. God called him *"a man after His own heart"* (1 Samuel 13:14), but that did not mean he makes no mistakes. The most important thing to God was that David knew how to find his way back to the heart of

God and no matter how many times he fell; he always managed to maintain his position in God's heart.

Peter had a better way of expressing this fire experience: *"Their purpose is to prove that your faith is genuine. Even gold, which can be destroyed, is tested by fire; and so your faith, which is much more precious than gold, must also be tested, so that it may endure. Then you will receive praise and glory and honor on the Day when Jesus Christ is revealed."* (1 Peter 1:7 - GNB). As a rock, he must have encountered the flames that tested his faith. It is in that testing of our faith that God manages to produce the rock that He can build His church upon. The gold, that we all want to have, has an experience with the fire. It is through the testing of the fire that whatever is not gold gets consumed and the genuine gold gets melted and separated from all

"The gold, that we all want to have, has an experience with the fire"

impurities. Because we come to the kingdom of God with all kinds of impurities, we also need a refining experience.

God showed His faithfulness to these words of the fire encounter that He speaks through Isaiah when the Hebrew lads encountered the same situation (Daniel 3). The only difference is that in their case, this was not figurative, it was a literal and real fire. Shadrach, Meshach and Abednego had an opportunity to face reality and waver in their faith, just like most of us often do when reality strikes. They were given another chance to deny their faith before they were thrown in the fire but they did not seize the opportunity to fall.

> "Because we come to the kingdom of God with all kinds of impurities, we also need a refining experience"

What amazed me about their situation is that they were also not sure that God will deliver them. This is their response: "*Shadrach, Meshach, and Abednego answered and said to the king, O Nebuchadnezzar, we have no need to return a word to you on this matter. If it is so that our God whom we serve is able to deliver us from the burning fiery furnace, then He will deliver us out of your hand, O king. But if not, let it be known to you, O king, that we will not serve your gods nor worship the golden image which you have set up."* (Daniel 3:16-18 - MKJV). They knew that God **can** save them but they did not know that He **will** at that time. They were ready to die for what they believed and God had a reason enough to walk with them in the fire, as the fourth man.

Sedimentary Rock

Sedimentary rocks are types of rock that are formed by the deposition of material at the earth's surface and within bodies of water (Wikipedia). The materials talked about here are little pieces of rocks that were cut off from the bigger rocks through the weathering process. These materials are called Sediments. Weathering is caused mainly by three things: **wind, water** and **ice.** The weathering process moves the sediments to a place where they settle. The wind can only carry certain masses of pieces of rocks and for a certain distance. The most powerful vehicle is water, because in its route it carries materials that are able to push others. Eventually the heavier sediments settle first and other sediments end up in the rivers and other water retaining structures. That is where they gather together to form a rock. Ice also causes weathering in the form of snow or hail by causing a severe reduction in temperature that can cause cracks in rocks and eventually melts to push the sediments as water. As these sediments become embedded, the gaps between them narrows and they eventually harden to form rocks.

Hebrews 10:25 says: *"Let us not give up the habit of meeting together, as some are doing. Instead, let us encourage one another all the more, since you see that the Day of the Lord is coming nearer."* (GNB). A Sedimentary rock is formed by pieces of rocks that come together. There is a special anointing that God places on the fellowship of the saints that releases the favour of God. As we come together we empower one

> *"There is a special anointing that God places on the fellowship of the saints that releases the favour of God"*

another and recharge one another. That is the purpose of church. It is more about the gathering of the saints. I have heard Christians say: "I don't need to go to church, I can read the bible on my own and I pray at home." Well that is not what the bible teaches us. In fact that is what the writer of Hebrews was concerned about. It was the habit of some Christians in those days to neglect the gathering of the saints, which is why it had to be mentioned. **The gathering is meant to produce a rock out of us!**

Take a careful look at Psalm 133: *"How wonderful it is, how pleasant, for God's people to live together in harmony! It is like the precious anointing oil running down from Aaron's head and beard, down to the collar of his robes. It is like the precious anointing oil running down from Aaron's head and beard, down to the collar of his robes. It is like the dew on Mount Hermon, falling on the hills of Zion. That is where the LORD has promised his blessing--- life that never ends."* (Psalm 133:1-3 - GNB). It is only three verses long but contains amazing revelations. First of all it highlights that it is wonderful and pleasant to have the fellowship of the saints. And then it shows the significance of this fellowship by giving comparing pictures. These are amazing pictures and I want us to observe them in detail.

The first picture is that of the oil poured on the priest's head. The priests used to be anointed with oil for their service to God and this anointing would qualify them for their service in the presence of God. One of the instructions that were to be carefully observed by the priests in those days is that they were not

> "We are all from the same God and we are connected by our faith in Jesus Christ"

allowed to cut off their beards. When the oil is poured on their heads, it comes from one point, which is the container, it scatters on the head and takes different directions on the head but then it comes together again at the beards. In essence it could indicate our relationship with God. We are all from the same God and we are connected by our faith in Jesus Christ. We might be saved in different places, at different times and on different occasions but we all form one body of Christ. The bible says that the church is the bride of Christ (Revelation 21:9) and one day we will be married to

Christ as one being, the church and bride of Christ. Our separation is momentary but our gathering has an eternal significance. I believe that every time we go to church we become empowered and refreshed. When we get out of church we are supposed to impact the world around us while we look forward to the next coming together for a fresh and new empowerment.

The second picture is that of the dew that falls on the mountains. I want us to concentrate on Mount Zion because it is mentioned a lot in the bible. Mount Zion was a sacred mountain to the children of Israel. It is the mountain that represented the presence of God. Psalm 9:11 says: *"Sing praises to the LORD, who sits enthroned in Zion! Tell among the peoples his deeds!"* (ESV). Whenever the children of Israel referred to this mountain, they were confident that God would answer their prayers. The fellowship of believers is likened to the dew that falls directly on the presence of God. This shows how valuable fellowship is. Jesus said: *"For where two or three are gathered together in my name, there am I in the midst of them."* (Matthew 18:20 -

KJV). Jesus assures us that He is just a fellowship away from us. That does not mean that He cannot attend to us individually, but there is somewhat a power released when we are together that He will not ignore our communion. The bible says two are better than one (Ecclesiastes 4:9).

As we herd previously from Jesus, a house that is built on a rock has great chances of survival against any hostile circumstance. The reason He brings us together to produce a rock out of us is because He desires to build His church on this rock. Christianity is not a one man show, it is a teamwork kind of lifestyle and God needs to be sure that He can count on us to reach out to the world out there. Just as the communities we live in are made up of a group of people, so God builds His church with a gathering of people. It is difficult for a Christian to survive alone. Starting with the act of receiving Christ in our lives, we need someone to share the Gospel with us. As Paul said in the book of Romans; *"So then, faith*

"...He can count on us to reach out to the world out there"

comes from hearing the message, and the message comes through preaching Christ." (Romans 10:7 - GNB). There is a lot that we can learn from each other that can reveal the nature and character of Christ that we need in order to live this godly life that we desire. The fellowship of the saints is one of the keys to producing a rock-solid Christian.

Metamorphic Rock

The word Metamorphism means *"Change in form."* It is a process through which metamorphic rocks are formed. Metamorphic rocks are formed from the transformation of existing rocks, which experience intense pressure and heat (Wikipedia). As the Igneous rocks and Sedimentary rocks on the surface of the earth sink deeper and deeper underground, they experience a greater amount of pressure from the soil and rocks above and on the sides. Heat starts to play a role when they get deep enough to approach the molten magma within the earth. Due to this intense pressure and heat, the rock becomes harder, with the particles within getting ever closely packed. Due to the change in environment, the rocks, which were in other forms, are forced to undergo a change through this process of Metamorphism.

Bessie Head, in her book, Maru writes: *"Environment everything, heredity nothing."* These words follow a discovery that the environment has a greater impact on a person so much that it can diminish the trace of the inherited background of the person's origin. The environment within which we live has an impact on who we become in the future. Before

> *"The environment within which we live has an impact on who we become in the future"*

God could do anything in Abram's life, He had to get him to a different environment first. The first words that Abram received from God were: *"...Get thee out of thy country, and from thy kindred, and from thy father's house, unto a land that I will shew thee:"* (Genesis 12:1 - KJV). Before Abram received anything else from God, he had to undergo a change of life and the only way his lifestyle could change was to have a different place to stay in.

Knowing Christ

As we already learned that in Christ we become a new creation (2 Corinthians 5:17), we cannot approach this new life in Christ with the old mindset. The only way we can embrace the newness of life is if we can think, feel and speak differently. Paul says to the Romans: *"And be not conformed to this world: but be ye transformed by the renewing of your mind, that ye may prove what is that good, and acceptable, and perfect, will of God."* (Romans 12:2 - KJV). The environment we live in affects the way we think and behave. This is because human beings have a nature of adapting. The best way to change our minds is to change our environment. This is the reason we are advised to change the people we hang around when we get born again. They played a huge role in us becoming what we were before we came to Christ. As long as we are with such people, we can never embrace the newness of life. That is what Paul meant by *"bad company corrupts good character."* (1 Corinthians 15:33).

"The best way to change our minds is to change our environment"

Since God is concerned about us becoming what He designed us to be, He allows a change of environment to come our way in order to bring us to the completion of

> *"Unfair as the situation seems, God is still at work within that environment, busy preparing us for the newness of life"*

His work in us. Sometimes the change of environment is not as literal as in the case of Abram, it comes in the form of pressure that makes us uncomfortable within the place where we are. For most of Christians, after giving our lives to Christ the people we were closest to rejected us because of our new faith. For some Christians, the old things we used to do felt uncomfortable and strange. These are some of the ways God allows a change of life to occur in us.

Some Christians went as deep as losing a lot of what they had. Unfair as the situation seems, God is still at work within that environment, busy preparing us for the newness of life. One man once said about Christianity: *"we are living an upstream life in a downstream world."*

The pressure is not meant to destroy us, it is meant to produce a rock out of us!

Paul says to the Corinthians: *"We are often troubled, but not crushed; sometimes in doubt, but never in despair; there are many enemies, but we are never without a friend; and though badly hurt at times, we are not destroyed."* (2 Corinthians 4:8-9 - GNB). The reality of the matter is that we sometimes go through tough times as children of God. It is not what we desire but we need the experience if we want to be

"...Irrespective of what we go through, He is still in control and working in our lives"

complete and become what God wants us to be. *"For it is God which worketh in you both to will and to do of his good pleasure."* (Philippians 2:13 - KJV). The most important thing both to us and to God is to trust Him with our lives that irrespective of what we go through, He is still in control and working in our lives. Failing to trust God is the greatest catastrophe in a Christian's life. We will become victims of worry, depression, unhappiness and fear.

The confidence that God is still with us in everything we go through keeps us alert of the enemy's attacks and helps us to remain firm, knowing that we are in a process of maturity towards perfection. **Nothing can ever happen to a child of God except God allows it and God only allows it if it will benefit us!** Paul assures us of this: *"There hath no temptation taken you but such as is common to man: but God is faithful, who will not suffer you to be tempted above that ye are able; but will with the temptation also make a way to escape, that ye may be able to bear it."* (1 Corinthians 10:13 - KJV). Firstly, what we go through is not beyond this world. It

"He promised that He will never leave us nor forsake us"

is common to man. Secondly, God is faithful. He promised that He will never leave us nor forsake us (Hebrews 13:5). The third thing is that He will never let us be tempted beyond what we can handle. Even though it does not feel that way when we go through it, the situation is not beyond what we can handle. Then lastly, He makes a way out for us that we may be able to endure. We do not have a reason to give up and give in! Paul says: *"For I reckon that the sufferings of this present time are not worthy to be compared with the glory which shall be revealed to us-ward."* (Romans 8:18 - KJV). He helps us to focus on the future while we go through the pressure. There is no other way to overcome the present unless we adopt the future mentality. Focusing on where we are going helps us to minimise the pressure and see it for what it really is, a temporary setting for a future glory.

Chapter 5:

The Benefit Of Testing

"Consider it a sheer gift, friends, when tests and challenges come at you from all sides. You know that under pressure, your faith-life is forced into the open and shows its true colors. So don't try to get out of anything prematurely. Let it do its work so you become mature and well-developed, not deficient in any way."
James 1:2-4 (MSG)

God is busy producing a rock out of our lives and He will do whatever it takes for us to become what He intends us to be. As we study all these different types of rocks, we see that the process of becoming a rock is not as easy as we can imagine when we see the finished product. However, there is no way the product can be produced without the process. Bishop Noel Jones, senior pastor of the City of Refuge Church, in his message "Come Forth" declared: *"Everything you are going through is just a setup, where God has created a situation in your life to set you up for a revelation of His word."* The most important thing is to reveal Christ to us, whether being it through situations, fellowship or a change of environment. Peter continues to say: *"For this is a gracious thing, when, mindful of God, one endures sorrows while suffering unjustly."* (1 Peter 2:19 - ESV). This unjust suffering is designed specifically to benefit you, to produce a rock that God can use for His glory. The most important thing to grasp in this suffering is that it has to do with God. Our own intentional suffering cannot be rewarded because it is not part of the plan and it does not produce the product of righteousness, it only shows us off to the world.

James says: *"My brethren, count it all joy when you fall into various trials, knowing that the testing of your faith produces patience. But let patience have its perfect work, that you may be perfect and complete, lacking nothing."* (James 1:2-4 - MKJV). Considering the experience of trials a pure joy somehow contradicts the state of our emotions. What James implies is that we should not respond to our emotions as much as we respond to our faith. Feelings are there to connect us to the state of our environment but faith connects us to the reality beyond our current state. I heard a statement in Impact Radio, one of the Christian Radio Stations in South Africa broadcasting in Pretoria, and this is what they said: *"Faith gives you real eyes to realise where the real lies."* As we learned previously, we cannot overcome the present state with our eyes fixed on the present. We need to project our eyes beyond what we are going through if we are to change our current situation. James tells us that trials produce perseverance. Perseverance is standing until the end. When you accept the mentality of perseverance, you acknowledge that there is an end to what you are going through. The bible tells us that: *"... Weeping may endure for a night, But joy comes in the morning."* (Psalm 30:5b - MKJV). No matter how long the night may seem, it can never keep the sun from shining the next day. This means that there is an end to trials just like there is always an end to the night in every new day.

> *"We need to project our eyes beyond what we are going through if we are to change our current situation"*

James continues to tell us that perseverance should finish its work in order to bring us to perfection. Somehow perseverance affects our character. That is the whole point of why God allows us to go through it. This is because our relationship with God has to affect our whole lives. In the process of making us more like Christ, God has to fix and tune our character to a godly character that can easily relate to Him. The bible teaches us that we should not remain spiritual babies forever; we need to grow and mature in our Christian living.

Maturity can only be reflected through character and character is developed by an encounter of different circumstances in different times. Paul says to the Corinthians: *"When I was a child, I spoke as a child, I understood as a child, I thought as a child; but when I became a man, I put away childish things."* (1Corinthians 13:11 - MKJV). There is a point where Paul had to put away childish things and I believe that point came with different experiences. When we were children we used to receive everything we desire by a simple weapon called crying. It was simple, when we want something we just cry out and the older person comes to our attention. Unfortunately we do not stay children forever and that is why we need a stage in our lives when we put away childish things. We need to grow up. The bible tells us that: "*...the earnest expectation of the creation eagerly waits for the revealing of the sons of God.*" (Romans 8:19 - MKJV). Sons are those who are able to take care of the inheritance, those who can make sure that the father's affairs are continually prosperous in the father's absence. That is where God wants us to be, in a stage where we are able to represent Him fully in this world.

Chapter 6:

Maturity and Responsibility

Knowing Christ

" When I was a child, I talked like a child, I thought like a child, I reasoned like a child. When I became a man, I put the ways of childhood behind me. " 1 Corinthians 13:11 (NIV)

A.

It is only when we are matured that we can be able to show the world who God is both through what we speak and how we behave. There is no short cut to maturity, the only way is through patient endurance. Galatians 4:1-2 says: *"Now I say that the heir, as long as he is a child, does not differ at all from a slave, though he is master of all, but is under guardians and stewards until the time appointed by the father."* (MKJV). I believe that one of the reasons we do not see the things that we desire and pray for come as soon as we desire is because we are not yet mature enough to can handle the responsibility that comes with them. After all,

> *"After all, God is our father and He knows us better than we know ourselves"*

God is our father and He knows us better than we know ourselves. Until such a time as we show the father that we are responsible enough, we still need to keep believing that the right time is coming. It is also applicable to our lives, as parents we promise our children things that are limited to a time frame. The time is often when we know that they are mature enough to handle the responsibility that comes with the promise. Somehow the understanding that we need to mature before we receive what we desire is what often motivates us to act and behave maturely, knowing that we are preparing for the reward.

This is what the book of Hebrews says: *"Therefore leaving the doctrine of the first principles of Christ, let us press on to perfection..."* (Hebrews 6:1a - WEB). We have already learned that perfection comes through maturity. When we reach the stage of maturity we know how to make things happen. We can always pray in line with the will of God because we know by experience what the will of God is (Romans12:2). There is nothing fulfilling to the father like having a mature son who is able to discuss serious matters that concern the family with him. One of the reasons Jesus was condemned by the Jews is because He called Himself the Son of God. God trusted Him with the affairs of Heaven, knowing that He will never back down from the plan when the going gets tough. He was a mature offspring of the Father. Having declared that He is the Son of God meant that He is at the state of equality with God; He can take the place of God and do what God can do. We saw the proof of that

> *"...A deep relationship with God releases power and authority in a person's life such that the extraordinary become ordinary to those that mature in Christ"*

through His ministry, when He did what normal human beings were unable to do. He commanded the storm to cease, he healed the sick through His words, demons fled at His command and the dead received resurrection through Him. This shows that a deep relationship with God releases power and authority in a person's life such that the extraordinary become ordinary to those that mature in Christ. In actual fact this was seen through the disciples who did exactly what Jesus did after He ascended. The same applies to us who choose to receive the promises of God by faith.

Jesus, in one of His parables teaches about a man who was going to a far country. (Matthew 25:14-28). This man gave to his servants, different amounts of talents, each one according to his ability. The first man receives five talents, the second man receives three talents and the third man receives only one. The first man multiplied his talents and so did the second man. The third man decided to hide his talent until the master came back so that he can give back what the master gave him.

These talents, according to the bible were an equivalent of more than fifteen years' wages of a labourer. Now it is easy for us to look at the third man and quickly judge him for not utilising his talents but I need us to look at things, perhaps the way he might have thought at that time. He had an equivalent of more than fifteen years' labourer's wages. The first thing that comes to mind is if he can try to multiply this money and end up losing it, he will never have any means of recovering it. The second thing is that for him to multiply it, he has to be exposed; there is a risk of robbery since people will know that he has the money. Having considered these things, I believe he saw it best to hide it rather than take a risk.

The only problem that I identify with this man is that he was given the money according to his potential but failed to produce. If the master did not know him he was not going to be in the list of those who receive talents. Knowing what he is capable of, the master entrusted him with a talent. Instead of believing that he has what it takes to multiply the gift, he must have looked at other possibilities and allowed a negative mind to overtake the possibility of multiplication. I can imagine when he received the talent, how exited he must have been, how overwhelming it was to realise that the master trusts him with his money, how many ideas ran across his mind with potential to utilise what he just received. That is what happens when we are quick to ask things from God yet we are not mature enough to handle them. We end up either squandering them, losing them over careless handling or hiding them instead of multiplying what God has entrusted to our care. God has to wait for us to mature enough for us to be able to take good care of His gifts and to maximise our potential as He knows we can. The process might be rough but if it will benefit us, we have to go through it.

It is the same with a father who takes a child to the dentist. After the cleaning or removal of the tooth, the pain is horrible and unbearable but the result has good returns that will last for a lifetime. If the tooth is not removed, the horrifying pain that comes as a result of the decay will be a permanent haunting pain in the baby's body. My friend and colleague, Pastor D.A. Mathala once preached a message that was entitled: *"Do not make permanent decisions in temporary situations."* In it he states that we often face situations that pressurise us to make quick decisions that can have irreversible consequences. We need to be sober enough to analyse the situation in order to avoid such a decision that can cost us more than we bargained for. He made mention of Hannah, who promised God the sacrifice of losing her child for the service of God in the temple (1Samuel

1:11). It was not really a bad decision she made but God is faithful and is able to change our situations even if we cannot afford the price of what it takes.

> *"Without going through some things in life, we will never value the gift of life"*

If she trusted the Lord enough, she would understand that it is not her promise that brings the child, it is God who opens the womb. This practice of a sober thinking comes with experience that pushes us to an analytical mode. Without going through some things in life, we will never value the gift of life. We will never be thankful for what we receive. We will never appreciate the little things that people do for us. We will never value the relationships that we have. We will never see the need of pushing ourselves to our maximum potential. The truth is that we need the challenges we face in our lives. If they were not necessary, we would have never met them.

Chapter 7:

Effective Life

"In faith there is enough light for those who want to believe and enough shadow for those who don't."
— *Blaise Pascal*

As a finished product, God wants us to live fruitful and effective lives. That is the purpose of all the process we have to go through to become the rock. Jesus says: *"...I have come that they may have life, and that they may have it more abundantly."* (John 10:10 - MKJV). If we are still not having abundant life, God is not done with us yet. If we are still unhappy with where we are God is still working on us. If what we have accomplished thus far does not feel sufficient, it means we have not yet reached the level of abundant life. That is what Christ came for us to have. The ultimate purpose is for us to live in abundance. If we still struggle to praise the Lord wholeheartedly within our environment, the Lord is still working on us. Until such a time as we see ourselves

"If we are still unhappy with where we are God is still working on us"

being able to praise the Lord in our working environment, pray freely in our spare time at home, walk in freedom within our community and greet everybody with a smile every day, we still need the process of maturity. That is what God desires to see in us. We need to reach a stage where our emotions do not control the state of our being but rather we, through the Word of God, are able to control our emotions to feel what God desires us to feel, to enjoy

"Until we are able to afford anything we need anytime, we still need to mature financially"

what the Word of God says, to take delight in the Word of God. That makes up the most part of abundant life. Until we are able to afford anything we need anytime, we still need to mature financially. We have not yet stepped in abundant life in that area. Until we live free from sickness and diseases, we have not yet reached abundant life; we need to mature in the healing power of God.

God wants us to live lives that represent Christ in this world. Jesus never used to worry about money. He had everything that he needed. In fact he had no need for money except maybe if He had to pay tax. The bible tells us that Judas, the man who betrayed Jesus, used to steal some of the money in the treasury (John 12:6). We never encountered a place where Jesus was short of money because of this man's behaviour, He always had all that he needed. That is the abundant life that I believe God wants us to live. If He ran short of food, He could multiply bread. He is the man that turned water into wine, the whine that was declared better that the first (John 2:3-10). He could have made a wine factory and kept on producing wine to sell. That was one of the things He was capable of. However, that was not the primary need in His life, He came to die for the sins of the world and that was the passion that was burning in His heart. We also need to live lives that pursue the God given passion in us without having hindrances that cost us to delay and lose focus. We need to reach a stage in our lives where we run after the

"We need to reach a stage in our lives where we run after the purpose of God without any crouching need that disturbs us"

purpose of God without any crouching need that disturbs us. That is why God has to allow us to mature until we know what matters the most and go for it. Until such a time as we live abundant lives, we still need God to work on us.

The knowledge of Christ is purposed to help us know who we ought to be in God. The more we seek to understand Jesus, the more we find the meaning of life and the more we find out the plan of God for our lives. There is a specific purpose why God brought us to this world in this generation and time. That is why we need God ever more because we could have been born in another time frame but we are here now. We need God to help us understand why we are here now. That can only happen if we seek Christ and God reveals to us our purpose in life. The knowledge of Christ establishes and matures our relationship with God. Jesus said to His followers: *""Many will say to Me in that day, 'Lord, Lord, have we not prophesied in Your*

> *"There is a specific purpose why God brought us to this world in this generation and time"*

name, cast out demons in Your name, and done many
wonders in Your name?'"And then I will declare to them,
'I never knew you; depart from Me, you who practice
lawlessness!'"* (Matthew 7:22-23 - MKJV). I was
amazed to learn that the word '**knew**' that He uses when
He says *"...I never **knew** you"* is the same word the bible
uses when it refers to people who are married. The bible
says: *"Now Adam **knew** Eve his wife, and she conceived
and bore Cain, and said, "I have acquired a man from
the Lord."'"* (Genesis 4:1 - MKJV). What Jesus implies is
that He will say in that that day: *"I never had an intimate
relationship with you."* This is the reason He said to His
disciples: *""Nevertheless do not rejoice in this, that the
spirits are subject to you, but rather rejoice because
your names are written in heaven." "* (Luke 10:20
MKJV).

The knowledge of Christ empowers us to do what Jesus
did. He says to His disciples: *""And these signs will
follow those who believe: In My name they will cast out
demons; they will speak with new tongues; "they will
take up serpents; and if they drink anything deadly, it*

will by no means hurt them; they will lay hands on the sick, and they will recover."" (Mark 16:17-18 - MKJV). These things are said to be done by those who believe. They are signs that we are believers in Christ. Jesus died on the Cross and rose again in power. There is a difference between power and authority. Power means the person has

> *"This power is released by the knowledge of Christ"*

what it takes to fulfil a task, whereas authority means the person does not have power but has a relationship with the one that has the power and as a result get the results that power produces without having the power. I believe we operate in authority while we are yet still immature in Christ.

However, the continual relationship with Jesus empowers us, until we start to operate in power. Peter says: *"As we know Jesus more His divine power gives us everything we need to live a godly life."* (2Peter1:3 - NLT). This power is released by the knowledge of Christ. The knowledge of Christ empowers us to cast out demons, it empowers us against sickness and diseases, it empowers us against our situations, it empowers us to be above and not beneath.

At the end of all things we need to be proper representatives of Christ in this world. If we are going to represent the kingdom of God then we need the resources of heaven to do it properly. We are the ambassadors of heaven. Whatever we have, whatever we need and whoever we are has to have a mark of heaven in it. When we read the Word of God we see that heaven is a place of more than enough. There is nothing lacking there.

If God wants to establish His kingdom on earth, He will ensure that the kingdom overflows just like heaven does. Our spiritual maturity brings us to that place where we have everything that we can ever desire yet without getting affected by the riches and wealth. Instead we focus on where God is taking us and ensure that our lives reflect the purpose for which God brought us to the earth.

"We are the ambassadors of heaven"

Spiritual Maturity means we do not react to the environment on the outside but we are able to listen and respond to the Spirit in spite of what is going on around us. We are blessed but we still serve the Lord. We are rich but we still pray and fast. We have all that we need but we still focus our energy on the will and purpose of God for our lives. That is our destiny while we are still here on earth, before we join the hosts of heaven in praising our father in His majesty and forever worship Him who sits on the throne. Amen.

NOTES

NOTES

About The Author

Pastor Katlego Clifford Malatsi is one of the pastors privileged to be part of the Born Fire Ministries, under the leadership of Bishop and Prophet Sefora. He received the Lord in his life at the age of 16 and ever since, God has been raising Him up to greater heights.

He is currently completing his studies of National Diploma, Civil Engineering with Tshwane University of Technology. He is married to Delisile Malatsi, and blessed with a baby boy, Salem. He is currently working together as a co-pastor with Pastor D.A. Mathala in the Mabopane Branch of Born Fire ministries.

To contact the author for speaking in your church or otherwise counselling:

Call: **(+27)73 065 6236** / email: **stakformal@yahoo.com**

www.ingramcontent.com/pod-product-compliance
Lightning Source LLC
Chambersburg PA
CBHW062022040426
42447CB00010B/2095